This 2021 edition was published by
Sovereign Noir Publications, LLC in Arlington, VA, USA.

All rights reserved. This book or any portion thereof may not be reproduced or used in any manner whatsoever without the express written permission of the publisher except for the use of brief quotations in a book review.

Cover Design by: Anthony K. Gervacio and KJH

Cover Art by: WikiImages

Hardback ISBN: 978-1-952987-10-6
Paperback ISBN: 978-1-952987-09-0
eBook ISBN: 978-1-952987-08-3

WOMAN.
QUEER.
BLACK.

KAMEISHA.
JERAE.
HODGE.

Woman.
Queer.
Black.

Kameisha Jerae Hodge

ACKNOWLEDGEMENTS

thank you so much.

    2020 was a year of tremendous beauty and ugliness, love and hatred, faith and doubt, pleasure and pain, and that was just in our personal lives. For Blacks, or those of the African Diaspora as a collective, it was another reminder that even during a global pandemic, the color of our skin made us susceptible to terrific anti-Blackness. Worldwide, we had to fight against oppressive and suppressive governments that did not have our best interests at heart—from Los Angeles to Lagos and London. Even within those fights of anti-Blackness, people still failed to see, understand, and acknowledge the intersectionality of folks' experiences. My soul still weeps for Black women who had not enjoyed the right to live their full lives. This book is for them. For you. For us.

    Let's do better. Live better. Demand better.

DEDICATION

This book is to serve as a constant reminder that Black women matter and is dedicated to every single Black woman in the universe. It's especially dedicated to every Black woman in my world.

From ancestors such as Queen Nandi and Queen Moremi, Harriet Tubman, Assata Shakur, Audre Lorde, Cicely Tyson, and Marsha P. Johnson to Megan Thee Stallion, Stacy Abrams, Taraji P. Henson, Yolonda D. Body, Briah Hash, Cici Gunn, and Breonna Taylor... this book is for them.

For my mama and my mama's mama.

For my sisters, aunties, and cousins.

For my nieces and daughters.

For my friends and mentees.

For my wife.

FORMATION

LET'S GET IN FORMATION:

DECONSTRUCTING RESPECTABILITY TO FIGHT FOR SOCIAL JUSTICE

Black literary traditions have "been largely divided between the slave narratives and abolitionist polemics of the antebellum era and the unique exfoliation of work in many genres that made up the era of the Harlem Renaissance," (Sundquist 105) according to *Nineteenth-Century Literature*. Indeed, primarily designed as a means to create an impenetrable voice for Black men and women in an age of sexism, racism, and classism bound together by capitalism, Black literary traditions can be easily argued that "the major force and greatest source of tension in Black writing... would be the question of 'assimilation'" (Sunquist 106). This sentiment reigns true. In select works from W.E.B. DuBois, Paul Lawrence Dunbar, Anna Julia Cooper, and Ida B. Wells-Barnett, each of these authors address 'assimilation' in their own ways; they attempt to thwart racism by deconstructing respectability politics and replace them with practical calls to action, and suggest combatting White Supremacy, racial oppression, and social justice through utilization of terminology such as 'wearing the mask,' 'double consciousness,' and 'intersectionality' to provide rationale for their activism.

Souls of Black Folk is a classic text wherein W.E.B. Du Bois talks about White Supremacy, anti-Black racism, the ways in which Black leaders have failed Black people, and what can be done to make some semblance of progress within the Black community. In critiquing how shortcomings from Black leaders have negatively impacted the fight for justice, Du Bois indubitably posits that it is impossible for Blacks in America to assimilate in a system that refuses to see and treat them as humans, let alone Americans.

Du Bois introduces the concept of the Veil and double consciousness – the Veil being a triple entendre that represents the blackness of Black people's skin, Blacks not being viewing themselves as true Americans, and others not seeing Blacks as true Americans whereas double consciousness is considered to be "…a peculiar sensation… [a] sense of always looking at one's self through the eyes of others, of measuring one's soul by the tape of a world that looks on in amused contempt and pity" (Du Bois 689). In putting a name to the *thing* that African Americans and other Blacks have experienced in this country – from slavery and Jim Crow to the Harlem Renaissance and the present – Du Bois went directly against the idea that they must strive to assimilate to White Supremacy in the United States.

He believes that Black leaders, such as Booker T. Washington, advocate too heavily to get Blacks to temporarily give up "political power," "civil rights," and "higher education of Negro youth" (Du Bois 699) when they should be fighting more than ever for the opposite. Du Bois' calls to action, instead, include shirking the mindset that Blacks need to follow the paths set for them according to Whites. He proposes that Historically Black Colleges and Universities need to be held to the same academic standards as White ones; that they must instill social activism and justice, strive to resolve the colorism issue globally, and develop men (Du Bois 724). Because he was of the belief that "African decolonization represented the vanguard of the struggle against white oppression" (Jones 24), it is of no surprise that this collection of essays infer that Du Bois is unapologetically Black and heavily encourages other Blacks to be the same way. He doesn't want to be dependent upon White America and feels that we should be able to take advantage of opportunities at White institutions whilst building our own.

In a similar vein, Paul Lawrence Dunbar's "We Wear the Mask" is a poem that ironically revels in the ability to use "social accommodationism" (Gates 895) to express how greatly it pains Black people to assimilate within a system that scrutinizes them that leaves them with "torn and broken hearts" (Dunbar 906) while simultaneous being mocked by the establishment "counting all their tears and sighs" (Dunbar 906).

Using the term 'wearing the mask,' Dunbar is referencing the degrading, dehumanizing way in which Black people often approach situations wherein they're forced to act in a certain manner. For example, Blacks must live in a state of duality. While sociologists call it "code switching" (Auer 3), Blacks approach speaking Standard Vernacular English during job interviews, in college classrooms, and at the workplace as a means of survival; it's generally frowned upon to speak African American Vernacular English or Black Vernacular English in any setting – from music videos to fiction – and is often brushed off as ghetto or unprofessional when any aspect of uncompromising Blackness is displayed. In order to be able to receive a diploma or degree, to get the job, or to maintain employment, Blacks literally have to "wear the mask," "smile," "grin and lie," and "sing" (Dunbar 906).

It can be argued that while Dunbar brings attention to the mask we wear, that he is not saying that Blacks should be complicit in doing so. He states that they have "mouths with myriad subtleties" (Dunbar 906) that should be used to create changes within the status quo. Along with Cooper and Du Bois, Dunbar likely wants Blacks to hold the United States accountable in its need to force Black Americans to not just assimilate, but to completely reject themselves in order to maintain White Supremacy, racism, and patriarchy (Eaves 25).

Anna Julia Cooper's "Womanhood a Vital Element in the Regeneration and Progress of a Race" makes a compelling argument that without investment in empowering, educating, and providing equality for

Black women, the state of Black America will remain stagnant and unyielding. Yes, Cooper articulates that while Black men strive to assimilate and acquire the privileges that White men receive, they should be more focused on getting Black women the same privileges that Black men have.

To challenge the notion that societal progress will only be solved by the eradication of racism, Cooper stated that "Only the BLACK WOMAN can say, 'when and where I enter, in the quiet, undisputed dignity of my womanhood, without violence and without suing or special patronage, then and there the whole Negro race enters with me." On the surface, this can be interpreted as a Black woman seemingly wanting to be treated fairly; however, it is much more complex than that. Historically, Black men have been fighting against racism for as long as Black women have. Black men have not historically been as willing to fight against patriarchy and sexism on behalf of Black women. She is essentially telling the Black community that she both acknowledges and abhors racism, however, as a Black woman, she has to fight an uphill battle of being discriminated against because of the color of her skin in addition to her genitalia.

Cooper brings up a very essential argument of intersectionality – that women of color, specifically Black women, have multiple oppressive levels that they have to endure. In saying that intersectionality matters, Cooper also acknowledges that while Black men had voting rights because of patriarchy (Newman 56) during the time, no man of her race should strive to be equal to White men until Black men treated Black women as their equals. A proposed solution that Cooper suggests is "developing Negro womanhood as an essential fundamental for the elevation of the race, and utilizing this agency in extending the work of the Church" (Cooper 630). By having the Black Church advocate for, and participate in, building leadership positions for Black women in religion, education, retail, corporate America, and other fields, Cooper believes that this would be the catalyst in propelling Blacks forward.

"A Red Record" is much more concise than all of the forms of Black literary traditions previously discussed. In essence, Ida B. Wells-Barnett does not rely heavily on rhetoric or anecdotal messages. Just as Anna Julia Cooper quotes prominent White leaders, Ida B. Wells-Barnett structures statistics and data from White people in such a way that their contradiction is evident. Additionally, she uses language that the everyday reader can understand and creates effective calls to action with both long-term and short-term solutions.

Wells-Barnett clearly articulates her two primary reasons for writing the text: to expose the supposed rationale behind the massive amounts of Whites who murdered Blacks during the Reconstruction Era, and to share records that prove White people's reprehensibility for continuing to reinforce White Supremacy and patriarchy

(Wells-Barnett 670). Thus, in no way, shape, or form did Wells-Barnett encourage assimilation. Like Paul Lawrence Dunbar, she too was all for accountability. Respectability politics had no place in her agenda, as can be seen via her five-point list that allows people the option to choose how to fight for social justice:

- "help disseminate the facts contained in this book," (Wells-Barnett 675)
- "[have] churches, missionary societies, YMCAs, WCTUs, and all Christian and moral forces in connection with your religious and social life pass resolutions of condemnation and protest every time a lynching takes place; and see that they are sent to the place where these outrages occur," (Wells-Barnett 675)
- "act and think on independent lines on this behalf, remembering that after all, it is the White man's civilization and the White man's government which are on trial," (Wells-Barnett 675)

- "[consider] the refusal of capital to invest where lawlessness and mob violence hold sway," (Wells-Barnett 675)
- "[send] resolutions to Congress indorsing Mr. Blair's bill and asking Congress to create the commission" (Wells-Barnett 675)

As can be seen, all of the writers ascribe to a standard wherein they approach assimilation and respectability politics with a ferocity that can only be described as Black literary tradition. They not only create terminology to change the way we frame the conversation of intersectionality, racism, and sexism, but they also collectively create multidimensional calls to action that appeal to different Black audiences.

According to Christopher E. Koy, professor of Mixed Race Studies at the University of West Bohemia, "In contemporary black fiction, the implications of the institution of slavery – the breakdown of the traditionally strong African families, the poverty of the majority of African Americans and the racism that still plagues America today – preponderantly find articulation" (Koy 2). While it is problematic that Black authors are expected to write solely about the aftermath of slavery in some form or another, Koy's observation holds merit.

In fact, the Black literary tradition of today still includes references to slavery, the Antebellum Era, Jim Crow, and the Harlem Renaissance. The only difference is that in deconstructing respectability politics and replacing them with practical calls to action, modern texts and contexts are used to build upon historic arguments.

Michelle Alexander begins her book, *The New Jim Crow*, accurately opens with the notion that "the more things change, the more they remain the same" (Alexander). In this text, Alexander makes a persuasive case that all of the discriminatory laws that were supposedly abandoned during the Jim Crow era were finagled to be legally applied to criminals.

Interestingly enough, a War on Drugs combined with rising crime in Black communities lead to an overwhelming amount of Black bodies in prisons. This assists Alexander in drawing the conclusion that "as a criminal, you have scarcely more rights, and arguably less respect, than a black man living in Alabama at the height of Jim Crow. We have not ended racial caste in America; we have merely redesigned it." (Alexander). In speaking out against systemic and institutionalized racism in America, Alexander is throwing respectability politics through window and, like Ida B. Wells-Barnett, is holding a mirror to this nation. Using statistics and data from resources such as the New York Times, the Central Intelligence Agency, and the Department of Justice, Alexander follows in the footsteps of Cooper and Du Bois by strategically utilizing information from the same system that seemingly seeks to destroy the Black community for good. She also begs the question of what

Black social justice activists are doing to alleviate this heavily racialized issue. Hint: the answer is *not much*.

Alexander, just like Du Bois and Cooper, believes that "a radical restructuring of our approach to racial justice advocacy is in order" (Alexander). She calls for "grassroots, bottom up" (Alexander) advocacy that ensures that all of the people – not just middle class Blacks or suburbanites – have a fair chance to experience prison reform, social justice reform, and civil rights organization reform (Alexander) without socioeconomic or racial bias.

Melissa Harris-Perry is the author of *Sister Citizen*, a book whose function "makes the claim that the internal, psychological, emotional, and personal experiences of Black women are inherently political" (Harris-Perry). Harris-Perry's argument is truly an amalgamation of Du Bois, Dunbar, and Wells-Barnett in that it speaks about the experiences of African Americans who struggle reconciling being Black and American. The twist, however, is that very much like Cooper, she uses "Black feminist tradition" alongside the Black literary tradition (Harris-Perry).

Harris-Perry deconstructed racism by using texts that White agencies and organizations have proclaimed to be literary classics to explain how America has an unconscionable need to "frame Black women in very narrow ways" (Harris-Perry). By analyzing and criticizing best-sellers such as *Their Eyes Were Watching God, for colored girls who considered suicide when the rainbow is enuf,* and *The Color Purple,* Harris-Perry is taking the time to pick apart why characters like Shug Avery are shamed when expressing their lasciviousness. She says very candidly that African American women should not have to wear a mask in order to prevent from being hypersexualized as either a Jezebel (Harris-Perry). Harris-Perry also talks in great depth about the disenfranchisement of African American women through the uses of the Mammy and Sapphire stereotypes, as well as Black liberation theology–a topic that Cooper herself touched on in "Womanhood a Vital Element in the Regeneration and Progress of a Race."

Drawing a poignant conclusion, Harris-Perry creates a call to action to two parties. The primary reader, the Black woman, is encouraged to watch other Black women's success and "be made taller by it, and use it to demand changes in the systems of racism and patriarchy that circumscribe American life" (Harris-Perry). It is important to note that she says *demand* instead of ask, request, or even beg. Harris-Perry wants Black women to see their own strength, too look around in solidarity, and to flip this system upside down Malcolm X style – by any means necessary. Her secondary reader, anyone who inquires about the state of Black women, is plainly told that Black women "want and need more than a fair distribution of resources: they also desire meaningful recognition of their humanity and uniqueness, and they are willing to make sacrifices to get it" (Harris-Perry). Simply put, give Black women resources, treat them like humans, and remember that just like any demographic, they are not a monolith. Every single Black woman is not the same, nor do Black women have a superhuman strength wherein they can keep being oppressed and still thrive. Black women want respect, justice, and fairness just like everyone else.

In ending, the idea that the Black literary traditions discussed in this essay, both past and present, still contain an unparalleled proximity to the pain found in texts such as *The Autobiography of Frederick Douglass*, *Incidents in the Life of a Slave Girl*, *We Real Cool*, and *Invisible Man* is both expected and disappointing.

It is expected in the sense that realistically, the trauma of being transplanted, treated as chattel, then being completely disrespected on the basis of skin color is not only ingrained in the psyche of Blacks in America, but it is literally passed down from generation to generation through anecdotes, poetry, academia, and literature–both fiction and nonfiction. The healing from four hundred years of slavery will not be done overnight. However, it is very disappointing that Black literary traditions are forced to expose the unsightly underbelly of American culture and history – the side that is consistently withheld from textbooks and grade school history classes. Racism and sexism, along with capitalism and White Supremacy, are all fundamentally the four chambers of America's heart. Black Americans are crucified whether they subscribe to what is deemed as appropriately dressed and "well-spoken", like Oprah, or whether they walk around topless in chains using African American Vernacular English like Tupac. It's bullshit, honestly.

Authors such as Cooper, Du Bois, Dunbar, and Wells-Barnett set the standards for tossing respectability to the side because they were aware of how Blackness works. They spoke absolutely and with great conviction about how to resuscitate the Black community. They took numbers and alternative facts that were meant to knock Blacks down, and threw them back to the establishment, and the people, with truth and fearlessness. Most importantly, they paved the way for authors from more recent generations – such as Michelle Alexander and Melissa Harris-Perry – to do the same. This begs the question of whether there will be a continued pattern of racial trauma instilled in Black literary tradition, or whether we will come to a point where we are healed enough to remember our past, and create a new Black literary tradition that doesn't have to hurt so much.

Works Cited

Alexander, Michelle. *The New Jim Crow*. The New Press, 2012. Kindle Edition.

Auer, Peter, ed. *Code-switching in conversation: Language, interaction and identity*. Routledge, 2013.

Cooper, Anna Julia. "Womanhood a Vital Element in the Regeneration and Progress of a Race." The Norton Anthology of African American Literature, edited by Henry Louis Gates and Valerie Smith, 3rd ed., vol. 1, W.W. Norton & Company, New York, 2014, pp. 618–633.

Du Bois, W.E.B.. "Souls of Black Folk." The Norton Anthology of African American Literature, edited by Henry Louis Gates and Valerie Smith, 3rd ed., vol. 1, W.W. Norton & Company, New York, 2014, pp. 687-760.

Dunbar, Paul Lawrence. "We Wear the Mask." The Norton Anthology of African American Literature, edited by Henry Louis Gates and Valerie Smith,

3rd ed., vol. 1, W.W. Norton & Company, New York, 2014, pp. 894-916.

Eaves, Latoya E. "We Wear the Mask." *Southeastern Geographer*, no. 1, 2016, p. 22.

Gates, Henry Louis, and Valerie Smith. "Ida B. Wells-Barnett." The Norton Anthology of African American Literature. 3rd ed. New York: W.W. Norton, 2014. 890. Print.

Harris-Perry, Melissa V. *Sister Citizen: Shame, Stereotypes, and Black Women in America*. Yale University Press, 2011. Kindle Edition.

Jones, David Colin. "Apart and a Part: Dissonance, Double Consciousness, and the Politics of Black Identity in African American Literature, 1946-1964." 2015.

Koy, Christopher E. "Reappraising the Black Literary Tradition [Special Issue]." *Litteraria Pragensia: Studies in Literature and Culture*, vol. 21, no. 41, July 2011, pp. 1-114.

Newman, Louise Michelle. White Women's Rights: The Racial Origins of Feminism in the United States. New York: Oxford UP, 1999. Print.

Sundquist, Eric J., and Dickson D. Bruce. "Nineteenth-Century Literature." *Nineteenth-Century Literature*, vol. 45, no. 1, 1990, pp. 105–107

Wells-Barnett, Ida. "A Red Record." The Norton Anthology of African American Literature, edited by Henry Louis Gates and Valerie Smith, 3rd ed., vol. 1, W.W. Norton & Company, New York, 2014, pp. 669-679.

INTERSECTIONALITY DON'T MATTER:

BLACK WOMEN'S THWARTED VOICES DURING SOCIAL MOVEMENTS

> *Oppressed groups are frequently placed in the situation of being listened to only if we frame our ideas in the language that is familiar to and comfortable for a dominant group. This requirement often changes the meaning of our ideas and works to elevate the ideas of dominant groups. In this volume, by placing African-American women's ideas in the center of analysis, I not only privilege those ideas but encourage White feminists, African-American men, and all others to investigate the similarities and differences among their own standpoints and those of African-American women.*
>
> - Patricia Hill Collins, Black Feminist Thought (vii)

In 2021, Black women represent a large amount of college degree holders – from associates to doctorates – yet, still earn only a fraction of the income that White men and White women receive. Even in a world where

Black women outperform Black men academically, we are still less likely to be hired over one, according to the Huffington Post (Bassett). This narrative of Black women coming in last in regard to these four categories is one that is neither new, nor unheard of. In fact, it has been in existence since our being imported to this country and extends far beyond things such as pay inequality and employment opportunities. We have participated in the creation of this country from the ground up, just like every other racial group, yet, despite the many ways in which Black women have stretched themselves in assisting with the progression of social justice, we have consistently been refused a seat at the philosophical table; Black women's voices have been intentionally drowned out of social justice movements — from the Women's Suffrage Movement, to the Civil Rights Movement, to the Black Power Movement, and, most recently, the Black Liberation Movement — because of our intersectional experiences as both Black citizens and women citizens, and our inability to value one identity over another. There was never a space created within those movements for Black women to safely voice their concerns and have those concerns pushed by the collective movement — so they created their own in response.

Before analysis, it is important to note the definition of intersectionality. Patricia Hill Collins, African American scholar and thought leader, is most famous for the theory that intersectionality is a critical component to Black feminist thought. As she stated in Black Feminist Thought: Knowledge, Consciousness, and the Politics of Empowerment, "Intersectionality refers to particular forms of intersecting oppressions, for example, intersections of race and gender, or of sexuality and nation. Intersectional paradigms remind us that oppression cannot be reduced to one fundamental type, and that oppressions work together in producing injustice." (Collins 18). This means that it is impossible for a Black woman to be able to divvy up her experience with oppression into neat categories because of multidimensionality. Take for instance the case of Sandra Bland, an African American activist who reportedly committed suicide while in police custody. When she was arrested for not putting out her cigarette, was it because she was Black, or because she was a woman? Was she pulled over because she was a Black woman, or was it because she was an activist who spoke out against White Supremacy and the criminalization of Black people? Because of her lived experience within all of those fundamentally different – and often opposing – paradigms that shape her existence, we will never truly know. Another important thing to remember about intersectionality is that it not only impacts the social, political, and economic ways in which Black women are oppressed and suppressed, but "the Venn diagram of race, sex and class and the dynamics of those intersections across two centuries has pushed African American women to the margins and erected a wall of invisibility from political discourse" (Locke 20).

Women's Suffrage Movement

What seems as simple as wanting all women to gain the same rights to vote as all men in the United States is not that simple at all. In fact, it has very little to do with gender and moreso to do with racism and upholding White Supremacy and all of its privileges.

The Women's Suffrage Movement initially began simultaneously while White women advocated for slaves and participated in abolitionist activism. Prior to this, however, they had gotten their voting rights stripped from them by the states and felt that they could relate to slaves being oppressed since they, too, could not vote (Newman 10). While this sounds great in theory, White women refused to see their privilege in unrealistically comparing themselves to slaves. The major difference between free and educated White women and Black slaves were literally White Supremacy. Based on this large gap in ability to understand the reality of the United States, it is understandable why the White leaders of the movement were not at all happy when their Black supporters, such as Frederick Douglass, had gotten the right to vote when they couldn't (Newman 6). In an article written in the London-based publication called The Telegraph, author and award-winning journalist Rahdika Sanghani reported that "American suffragette Carrie Chapman Catt, founder of the League of Women Voters, is known to have said: 'White supremacy will be strengthened, not weakened, by women's suffrage." She continued to report that, "While Rebecca Ann Latimer Felton, the first woman to serve in the Senate, said: 'I do not want to see a negro man walk to the polls and vote on who should handle my tax money, while I myself cannot vote at all.'" (Sanghani). This withdrawal from allyship among Blacks was not just relegated to those women, either; champion suffragette Susan B. Anthony also was not willing to continue to work with Blacks holistically to receive women's voting rights.

> *More than just a strategy to keep the woman's movement focused on a single issue, Anthony's efforts to avoid this particular controversy reveal how white activists worked to develop specific relationships among race, gender, and equality: that is, to establish the white woman as the primary definer and beneficiary of woman's rights at a time when the country was growing increasingly hostile toward attempts to redress the political, social, and economic injustices to which African Americans were subjected. White women's expressions of resentment over the enfranchisement of black men and these women's subsequent decision to keep the movement clear of "race" questions were part of a larger post-Reconstruction retreat from support of racial justice.* (Newman 5)

Meanwhile, Black women were cognizant of the continued racial tension and continued to fight for women's suffrage and abolition. White women discouraged Black women from participating in the National American Women Suffrage Association (NAWSA) and did not welcome them, White women did not allow Black women's suffrage clubs – such as the National Association of Colored Women, the National Council of Negro Women, and the Alpha Suffrage Club of Chicago – to affiliate with the NAWSA, and White women forced Black women to march in a segregated unit during the Suffrage Parade of 1913 ("African American Women and Suffrage").

These are just a few ways in which Black women were silenced and not shown appreciation during this fight. During most of the meetings, White feminists "were not truly interested in change, but finding their place in the existing system, using the same ideologies, thoughts and strategies of patriarchy that ignored the differences of women of color" (Locke 20). During the Women's Suffrage Movement, White women didn't care to particularly understand the more difficult experience of how gender and race simultaneously caused a completely different experience for Black women during the time. In this movement, Whiteness trumped Blackness, and thus

Black women were still forced to march in segregated parades and rallies. Their intersectionality and voices were not appreciated in that space, so they created their own by creating Black Feminism, Womanism, and Black feminist organizations.

Black women who were a significant, but invisible, part of the suffrage movement are: Sojourner Truth, Ida Bell Wells-Barnett, Mary Eliza Church Terrell, Mary Ann Shadd Cary, Nanie Helen Burroughs, Frances Ellen Watkins Harper, Juanita Craft, and Daisy Elizabeth Adams Lampkin ("African American Women and Suffrage;" Frear). It is also important to note that while the 19th amendment was passed, most Black women were still disenfranchised when it came to voting; thus proving that intersectionality was a very important conversation that needed to be had.

Civil Rights and the Black Power Movement
From the 1950s to the 1960s, Blacks successfully

created the "largest social movement of the 20th century" (Davis) leading to legislative and federal changes in the way Blacks were explicitly treated. Prior to this, White Supremacists masked as 'good White folks' such as J. W. Milam and Carolyn and Roy Bryant were able to lie under oath, beat, torture, shoot, and discard the bodies of Black people without getting charged ("Black Lives, White Lies and Emmitt Till"). It wasn't just the Ku Klux Klan that Blacks were fighting against; they were fighting against law enforcement who regularly attacked peaceful protesters with teargas, high pressure water hose, and fire dogs accompanied by riot gear in Selma, Alabama (Harmon). They were fighting other legislature that allowed for them to be denied services and products, equal public health care and education, and unfair trials with unjust legal counsel. They were fighting against literacy tests that were both illogical and impossible to pass, along with other voter disenfranchisement such as intimidation and gerrymandering (Harmon). In short, because of White Supremacy on every level of the judicial system, the Civil Rights Movement became a way for Black people in America to peacefully and demonstrably protest racism in all its forms (Davis).

During this same time, the Black Power Movement was also becoming a nationwide trend. The contempt for Blacks shown explicitly by local, state, and federal governments throughout the aforementioned systems of oppression was the main reason that Blacks were in need of a collective sense of empowerment and protection.

That's where the Black Power Movement comes in. It was created as a call "for armed struggle announced by the Black Panthers, and inspire[d] the poetry and race consciousness of the Black Arts Movement… a political revolution with an army of the Black underclass" (Joseph xvii). While it radicalized the quest for peace, it also created tension between those who were hung up on respectability politics and those who were fed up with have to beg for freedom.

It did a lot for the Black community in that they provided resources, security, and support that the government would continually deny them. The Black Power Movement, run by the Black Panthers, gave food to those in need, patrolled communities to decrease gang and police infested neighborhoods, maintained peace among Blacks, encouraged financial and economic separatism since the current capitalist society only benefitted White people. While many of the projects to create housing for Black people without living arrangements — such as Project MOVE — were destroyed by government officials (Wagner-Pacifi 2). For some reason or another, as found in the Tulsa bombings, the government and White citizens did not like the idea of a prolific Black community and literally bombed these communities while simultaneously arresting all of the movement's leaders and participants. The Federal Bureau of Investigations (FBI) even got involved.

During both of these movements, Black women attempted to include their unique experiences within the agenda for combating White Supremacy in their lives, however, still, they were not heard.

When it came to the Civil Rights Movement, women such as Septima Poinsette Clark, McCree Harris, Shirley Sherrod, Thelma Glass, and Johnnie Carr were often the ones who initiated protests, formulated strategies and tactics, and mobilized other resources (especially money, personnel, and communication networks) necessary for successful collective action" (Barnett 163). Yet, most of the Civil Rights leaders that we are introduced to are Martin Luther King, Jr., Malcolm X, Thurgood Marshall, W.E.B. DuBois, Stokely Carmichael, Bayard Rustin, and perhaps Rosa Parks and Mary McLeod Bethune. During this movement, as well as the Black Power Movement, "much of the movement was indeed deeply macho in orientation and treated women in many of these groups in a distinctly secondary and disrespectful fashion… for men who, often for the first time in their lives, exercised extraordinary power over others, sexism became a tool of sexual dominance over subordinates" (Mumia 173). Power, as a very structured dynamic, was extremely present because at the core of Black power and equality was the desire to maintain patriarchal privilege. Just as in the case of women's suffrage, Black men did not cape for Black women's rights. So when it came to Black women's voices, experiences, and leadership being important, their "roles have virtually been neglected, forgotten, or considered inconsequential or of secondary importance relative to those of men" (Barnett 163).

Black Lives Matter / Black Liberation Movement

The Black Lives Matter / Black Liberation Movement was created in response to the criminalization of Black victims of police brutality and the White Supremacy prominent in the criminal justice system. In fact, the website explicitly states the mission of the BLM Movement. It is as follows:

Black Lives Matter is a unique contribution that goes beyond extrajudicial killings of Black people by police and vigilantes. It goes beyond the narrow nationalism that can be prevalent within some Black communities, which merely call on Black people to love Black, live Black and buy Black, keeping straight cis Black men in the front of the movement while our sisters, queer and trans and disabled folk take up roles in the background or not at all. Black Lives Matter affirms the lives of Black queer and trans folks, disabled folks, Black-undocumented folks, folks with records, women and all Black lives along the gender spectrum. It centers those that have been marginalized within Black liberation movements. It is a tactic to (re)build the Black liberation movement. (Cullors, et al.)

The unfortunate part of the Black Lives Matter / Black Liberation Movement is that without research or prior knowledge, one would think that it was created by Black men; after all, it was founded and produced after the death of Trayvon Martin — a Black teenaged male who was murdered because George Zimmerman thought he looked like a possible threat to the community. BLM was there — peacefully protesting. When Michael Brown was murdered by a police officer after being left on the street for four hours, as well as being demonized as a thug and "demon" posthumously, BLM was right there protesting and being teargassed. When Eric Garner was choked to death by a police officer, BLM flooded the streets and begged for the officers to be charged with excessive force. They protested for Walter Scott. Tamir Rice. Alton Sterling. While all of these boys and men were killed at the hands of either neighborhood watch or police officers within minutes, it shows that White Supremacy still deems Black lives as disposable.

As Locke points out, "If the gendering of police violence is seen as a social problem that focuses only on African American men, then that means a large constituency group in the American political system does not exist for policymakers" (Locke 22). While the movement claims to "center those who have been marginalized within Black Liberation movements" (Cullors, et al.), it certainly seems that the same Black queer and trans folk, disabled folks, Black-undocumented folks, folks with records, and women that they claim to support and affirm are not part of their actual agenda. There was no BLM march for Tanisha Anderson or Yvette Smith. There was no protest on behalf of Shelly Frey, Darnisha Harris, Malissa Williams, or Alesia Thomas. Incidentally enough, African American women — trans, hetero, cis, queer, and otherwise — are largely ignored, despite being the sole developers of this movement.

Rising concern over the lack of voices for Black women and girls who were killed by police drove other Black women to create #SayHerName, a social media resistance. Black women who were able to distinguish intersectionality and how Black women are *also* representative of Black lives mattering wanted to pay their respects to those who have died at the hands of police brutality as well (Barnett 167); yet, when it comes to #SayHerName, Black women have been accused of trying to detract from the Black Lives Matter movement. The misconception here is that Black Lives Matter movement, because of how they have operated in the world, is to be solely about Black boys and men who have been unjustly killed by law enforcement. As much as the founders say otherwise, there is no indication that these perceptions are false.

Conclusion

Black women have always been at the forefront of social justice movements, from the Women's Suffrage Movement and to the Civil Rights and Black Power Movements of the 1950s and 1960s to the modern day Black Liberation Movement. Whether it was pushing race to the side and fight to benefit White women's privilege, or casting gender aside to fight for Black men's patriarchal privilege, it seems that no matter what Black women did, no demographic was willing consider their multidimensionality and fight for them.

Black Suffragettes such as Sojourner Truth, Ida Bell

Wells-Barnett, Mary Eliza Church Terrell, Mary Ann Shadd Cary, Nanie Helen Burroughs, Frances Ellen Watkins Harper, Juanita Craft, and Daisy Elizabeth Adams Lampkin were disregarded for more palatable, White activists such as Susan B. Anthony and Carrie Chapman Catt. Black women who fought for Civil Rights and Black Power such as Septima Poinsette Clark, McCree Harris, Shirley Sherrod, Thelma Glass, and Johnnie Carr are overlooked and unmentioned while Martin Luther King, Jr., Malcolm X, Thurgood Marshall, W.E.B. DuBois, Stokely Carmichael, and Bayard Rustin are praised beyond reconciliation. Even in death, neither Shelly Frey, Darnisha Harris, Malissa Williams, nor Alesia Thomas were mentioned nearly as much as Trayvon Martin, Michael Brown, Walter Scott, Tamir Rice, Eric Garner, or Alton Sterling.

It is absolutely clear that when it comes to Black women, their only allies are themselves. Their voices and experiences were denied in liberal, so-called progressive movements. They were not seen as valuable participants in the fight for justice, as they were forced to create reactionary safe spaces — namely the National Association of Colored Women, the National Council of Negro Women, the Alpha Suffrage Club of Chicago, Black Feminism, Womanism, and #SayHerName — where they were not forced to choose between their identities. Perhaps in the future, when the fight for equity is truly being sought, Black women will be included in the revolution. More than likely, we will even lead it.

Works Cited

"African American Women and Suffrage." *Rights for Women: The Suffrage Movement and Its Leaders*. National Women's History Museum, 2007. Web. 30 Jan. 2017.

Barnett, Bernice McNair. "Invisible southern black women leaders in the civil rights movement: The triple constraints of gender, race, and class." Gender & Society 7.2 (1993): 162-182.

Bassett, Laura. "Black Women Are The Only Demographic Not Gaining Jobs." The Huffington Post. TheHuffingtonPost.com, 5 Sept. 14. Web. 30 Jan. 2017.

"Black Lives, White Lies and Emmitt Till." *The New York Times*. The New York Times Company, 6 Feb. 2017. Web. 6 Feb. 2017.

Collins, Patricia Hill. Black Feminist Thought: Knowledge, Consciousness, and the Politics of Empowerment. New York: Routledge, 2000. Print.

Cullors, Patrisse, Garza, Alicia, and Tometi, Opal. and Alicia Garza. "About the Black Lives Matter Network." Black Lives Matter. Black Lives Matter Online, 2012. Web.

Davis, Jack E. "Civil Rights Movement." Grolier Multimedia Encyclopedia. Grolier Online, 2014. Web. 08 Aug. 2016.

Frear, Yvonne. "Making the Invisible, Visible: Juanita Craft and Grassroots Activism in the Civil Rights Movement in Dallas, Texas" Paper presented at the annual meeting of the 95th Annual Convention, Raleigh Convention Center, Raleigh, North Carolina. 27 Nov. 2014. Web. 08 Aug. 2016.

Harmon, Rick. "Timeline: The Selma-to-Montgomery marches." *USA Today.* Gannett Satellite Information Network, 06 Mar. 2015. Web. 06 Feb. 2017.

Joseph, Peniel E. *Waiting 'til the midnight hour: A narrative history of Black power in America.*

London: Macmillan, 2007.

Locke, Mamie. "The Invisibility of African American Women in Political Discourse of the Black Lives Matter Campaign." Virginia Social Science Journal 51 (2016): 17-25.

Mumia, Abu-Jamal. We Want Freedom: A Life in the Black Panther Party. Cambridge, MA: South End Press, 2004. Print.

Newman, Louise Michelle. White Women's Rights: The Racial Origins of Feminism in the United States. New York: Oxford UP, 1999. Print.

Sanghani, Radhika. "The Uncomfortable Truth about Racism and the Suffragettes." The Telegraph. Telegraph Media Group, 06 Oct. 2015. Web. 08 Aug. 2016.

Wagner-Pacifici, Robin. *Discourse and destruction: The city of Philadelphia versus MOVE*. University of Chicago Press, 1994.

WOMAN. QUEER. BLACK.

DISCOUNTED

My brother was 23.
Biggie was 24.
Tupac was 25.
There's no coincidence;
all these mothers still mourn
in public
and in private.
Their cases are still unsolved,
with no hope of finding closure,
yet
niggas still wonder why
Black lives don't matter.

SUPERNOVAE

I don't want to be a martyr
And I certainly
Don't want my death to be a
Grain in the sands of time

Let my love
And literature last
For lifetimes
So that those
Hiding in the shadows
Of fear
And doubt
Can see

The truth
And the light

WHITE DWARF

I have hundreds
Of thousands of years
Of the ancestors' wisdom
Coursing through my anatomy—
Both physiologically
And metaphysically.

Don't ever get it twisted.

ABSOLUTE ZERO

She feeds the dust of your ancestors
To your poisoned seed,
And yet you
Ostracize her for
The way she swaddles the
Universe in her arms
While balancing the World
On her back.

How dare you ask
The sun to be the moon
Simply because it shines too brightly,
Or for the moon to be the sun
Simply because it raises the tides
That crash against your
Hollow patriarchy.

KAMEISHA JERAE HODGE

AFFIRMATION

I'm a boss, literally,
and I live a life of abundance
that I cannot possibly conceive.

I am finally free.

JUSTICE OR JUST US

Convict the murderers
of Breonna Taylor—

Jonathan Mattingly
Brett Hankison
Myles Cosgrove

Periodt.

That's it.

That's the poem.

COUNTER FORFEIT

I'd never tell you
That your weakness is my strength
How much your absence
Makes me more present
Than I ever thought possible

I'd never tell you
That you were all I wanted
Yet you kept me at arm's length
While the others kept your attention

No

I'd never tell you that you're the reason
I distrust men
And that I have a hard time being
Comfortable around them
Ever since grandma died

I'd never tell you
Not because you're not worth the breath
It takes to make myself feel small
But because you never cared enough
To even ask

BEAUTIFUL

I remember looking at you
Seeing your smile for the first time
Thinking that you were going to be
The thing that saved me
From myself

And you did
And you were
And you are

And you still...

BITTERSWEET

Her lips were honey
And when I said her name
in a mirror
three times
Her love stung me terribly
Like Candyman meets
My Girl

TWIN FLAME

I swear
When the Universe
Made us
It knew that
We were
Far too powerful
And took us
Down a notch
By splitting us
Like atoms

TROPOSPHERE

WHOSE STORY IS THIS ANYWAY?

My mother is a single parent and has two sisters. At a very young age, my mom made it a point to explain to me the importance of educational, spiritual, and financial independence. She wanted me to be able to go to school and better myself, be able to decide whether I wanted to take part in Christianity (despite its inherit patriarchy, sexism, and misogyny), and be able to pay all of my bills on my own. Her goal was to make sure that I never needed to depend on a male for anything.

My paternal grandfather sought to teach me the same thing, however, his methodology was completely different. Under the guise of self-sufficiency, he essentially molded me into a housewife. I learned how to cook full-course meals, as well as which products clean the best. By the time I was 12, I had learned over a hundred uses for WD-40. I also knew how to degrease an oven, defrost a deep freezer, plaster and paint holes in walls, and snake a toilet. The majority of my family is old-fashioned and ascribe to very heterosexual, patriarchal traditions. Everyone assumed that I would become a Christian woman and marry a Christian man to carry on the family name. Because I wore sweatpants and fussed over dressing "girly," my family pegged me as a tomboy and assumed I would grow out of it.

My peers weren't very much different. Because I excelled in gym and was athletic, many of them associated me with being a lesbian or tomboy. I always played basketball, football, and tag with the boys in the neighborhood, but I would also play hand games with the girls, too. There was an obvious gender role that young boys and young girls played–and still do now–that I never cared to participate in. The boys liked to be aggressive and active. The girls wouldn't do anything for fear of getting dirty. They acted the same way that women did on TV shows such as I Love Lucy and Leave it to Beaver; they pined over guys who were focused on their careers and wanted their dinner to be ready by the time they got home. Many of the girls in my life, who eventually became women, obsessed over making themselves more suitable for a potential husband. From advertisements to movies and magazines, gender roles had always made women out to be overly emotional and overly concerned about other people's perceptions of them whereas males were taught to be independent and to influence what others think. Being subject to those people in those environments, I began to want those things too. How dangerous that is... to be moved to believe that you want something when in reality, you simply don't. On the other hand, once I truly found myself, I made career and educational moves solely to discover more about myself and to be able to purchase the equity and assets I wanted in life.

As a Black woman, I've always had to reconcile being a victim of racism from White Supremacists and bigots, as well as a victim of sexism from patriarchs, White

Supremacists, and Black men. No matter how many accomplishments I've had, how many degrees I've received, the number of books I've published, or how many youth I've mentored, it seems like, in this country, I will always be judged by the kinkiness of my hair. The amount of melanin in my skin. The fullness of my lips. Whether my body conforms to a stereotype based on my genitalia – whether the clothes I wear appropriately reflects the gender I was assigned at birth.

I am paid significantly less than my White peers - especially when I have more experience in a field that I've been studying since I was fourteen years old. I was assumed to have been on an athletic scholarship when I attended a private, predominantly White college in undergrad. I have been molested by four males in my family. I was sexually assaulted by my one of my best friends' partners. I am catcalled and harassed on the street for who I unapologetically am.

Based on the intersectionality of my gender, race, and sexuality, my gender identity is a queer, masculine presenting female. Most people who don't know me assume that I have some sort of hang-up regarding my body or self-esteem because I am very feminine in the way I speak and other non-physical mannerisms, yet, I wear sweats or basketball shorts by default. I in no way think or feel that I am a male; however, I am aware that my expression of gender can vary between being a selfless housewife like June Cleaver and being able to manicure the lawn or work all day like Ward Cleaver. My gender identity doesn't allow me to just be hyper feminine or hyper masculine. I'm able to bring home the bacon AND cook it, and anyone who has a problem with me living my truth can go straight to hell.

WOMAN. QUEER. BLACK.

BLUE MOON

Perfection personified
Classiness codified
Everything you wanted
And desired
Right before your eyes

Ineffectively eroticized
Unpretentiously prophesied
I am what your wildest
Dreams and nightmares
Are without compromise

LIGHT POLLUTION

Mama said be home 'fore the
Lamp posts came on
But she never said what to do
When the fake candles
Ran out of batteries
And the monsters crawled
Out of your gene pool,
Lapping around your body
Like police cars
When the weekends came up

CUSP

Before,
because I was broken,
I chased desire with abandon and
hopeless irresponsibility with no intent
of knowing
who I was
or who I would be.

Now,
I've found
an unconditional thing
inclusive of heretic curiosity and
genuine admiration
as I search for
myself eternally.

TRINITY

I never hear you.
Footsteps as heavy as a slaughtered lamb
carried to the alter for sacrifice,
your prints don't leave themselves
in the sand (despite your burdensome load).
I may as well be deaf.

I never feel you.
Philanges strong and sacred,
yet, sacriligous enough to silently sin.
Soft enough to still my speaking in tongues,
smart enough to curl themselves within me.
I may as well be paralyzed.

I never see you.
Eyes judiciously steering me in the way,
the truth, and the life, you are never unjust.
I know you are there,
guiding my actions and speech,
to ensure that I'm not ensnared in the fall of man.
I may as well be blind.

You say my worship is pure.
I say my worship is hypocrisy.

GOODNIGHT, SWEET MOON

during the day,
the sun almost outshines
out dances
out performs those confident curves-
the holes within-
that you can't hide from.
we see you in the background
providing a lunar yin
to a solar yang.
however,
throughout the night,
your cup runneth over
like a drinking gourd.
silently
judiciously
audaciously
bringing her children home
toward freedom.
you become both a moon and
the center of an entire universe
once you refuse to dim
your light.

THE BALL BOY

waiting.
wishing.
wondering when i'll have my chance to
surveil audiences
from sydney to sacramento,
failing to understand why-
despite the hands i strategically place behind me-
i have continued to break my fingers
by lifting your spineless back.
i wonder if it's worth the humiliation
of being seen
and not heard.

RETROGRADE

we've fallen victim
to carelessness
again.
but, unlike last time,
shame is a harder pill to swallow
than admitting my wrongs.
i wear my mistakes; they're branded
on my chest
like a scarlet letter.
in time, the scabs
will crust over and peel, but, for now,
these freshly carved wounds
hurt worse than anything else.

TWILIGHT

conversations;
verbal sparring about
abstract theories
and concrete feelings
and where on the spectrum of truth
they lie

conversations;
debates turn emotional fallacies
into limited debacles-
however embarrassing
the end result may be,
knowledge is always gained
and insight is outsourced

IRREGULAR

there are some remnants
of hope
right there
where my heart used to be-
before your selflessness broke us
and my selfishness
smothered us
and our clawing
through sheets of oceanic ice
almost prevented us
from drowning.
now i watch us fall like birds
with wings crippled by the weight
of the world's sins.
we were each others' kryptonite.

and still are.

MEMORIES

i remember this ache-
this burning lump in throat from
refusing to vomit
the wrong words,
this hot singe of my tear ducts that
threatens to dry my
eyes permanently,
this throbbing ache
wherein my entire heart
collapses around itself...

simply because i
ain't strong enough to be
who you want me to be.
i can't cut people off like Kunta's foot
or Johnny Boy's penis or Ekua's clitoris;
life is already too hard,
and i won't force people
to endure their journeys alone.

COSMOS

THE COLOR PURPLE

In the film The Color Purple, which was adapted from Alice Walker's bestselling novel, gender expression is used through the bodies of Celie and Nettie. The use of their bodies is indicative of how African Americans have internalized society's perception of the lack of dominion Black women have over their bodies.

Celie and Nettie are sisters - the former being described as "black, poor, a woman, nothing at all," (Walker/Spielberg) and the latter being sexually coveted by both her father and her brother-in-law due to her beauty. Celie and Nettie are both dark skinned and wear natural hair. While clearly the only difference between Celie and Nettie is Nettie's conviction and outspoken demeanor, all of the Black males of authority in the film - specifically her father, her husband Albert, and her father-in-law Old Mister - consistently treat her as a workhorse and speak ill of her. A very disturbing example of this is when her father sets up her marriage with Albert. Albert initially wants to marry Nettie, but settled for Celie as an unwanted second option. Celie has no decision in the matter, whatsoever. The dialogue in that particular scene is as follows:

> "I can't let you have Nettie. She too young, but I'll tell you what - I'll let you have Celie. She the oldest anyhow, she ought to marry first. She ain't fresh, but I 'spects you know that. She's spoiled. Twice. Celie's ugly but she ain't no stranger to hard work. God done fixed her. You can do anything you want to do with her and she ain't gonna make you feed it. But Nettie, you flat out can't have, not now, not never." (Walker/Spielberg)

It is clear that there is a sort of value system that exists within the film, that being that bodies that have borne children aren't worth respecting or wanting. At the same time, virginity and youth are very desirable. With her father's consent, Albert verbally, physically, and mentally abuses Celie, including using rape, throughout the duration of their marriage. Despite her father's wishes, however, Albert attempts to rape Nettie while still being married to Celie. When she fights him, he drags her off the property and bans her from contacting her sister.

We see here that there is an obvious indication that even during a time when Black people as a whole are being oppressed, Black women are still the most dispensable people. They have to deal with being subject to prison or death at the whim of White people, but based on their physicality, may be subject to rape or abuse by Black men and/or women as well. Women's bodies in the film are treated as child bearing, house cleaning, sex machines. Even upon liberating herself, as most of the women in the film do, Celie gave Albert a part of her mind. When she leaves him to live with her best friend, or lover, as the novel implies, Albert responds, "You ugly, you skinny, you shaped funny, ain't nobody foolish enough to marry you. All you fit to do is be Shug's maid! Maybe take out her slop jar and maybe cook her food, but you ain't that good of a cook anyway." (Walker/Spielberg)

I think the message that Walker and Spielberg try to express is that patriarchy is just as evident in Black society as it is in a White Supremacist one, and that the effects are unequivocally devastating to Black women. In this film alone, a father rapes his daughter twice, and impregnates her, then gives her baby Olivia away before handing over her daughter's freedom to another man. Next, this new guy comes along and treats his wife and sister in law like the scum of the earth, even going as far as letting his mistress stay in the same house with them when she's in town. The story itself takes gender, power, and will and converts it into a magnificent piece of art that imitates life in the worst and most beautiful ways.

Works Cited

Spielberg, Steven, Kathleen Kennedy, Frank Marshall, Quincy Jones, Menno Meyjes, Danny Glover, Adolph Caesar, Margaret Avery, Rae D. Chong, Whoopi Goldberg, Oprah Winfrey, Allen Daviau, J. M. Riva, Michael Kahn, and Alice Walker. *The Color Purple*. Burbank, CA: Warner Home Video, 2003.

Walker, Alice. *The Color Purple: A Novel*. Penguin Books, 2019.

WOMAN. QUEER. BLACK.

IMPLOSION

the flowers you bought me-
the bouquet with the
assorted fragrances that
blossomed like
the sugary sweetness of springtime-
they've died.

one day they were vibrant
filled with life
and its beauteous splendor.
when i glanced back
they were limp and ill watered,
petals lie lifeless
on the stovetop
and stems were as broken as
the promises we made
to one another.

they no longer tickle my
nostrils with scents of forgiveness;
they only remind me of how
we've made a competition
of hurting one another.

WOMAN. QUEER. BLACK.

despite the impending death
looming over them
like distant lovers,
i kept them in memory of you.
i kept them in memory of
my effort to keep fighting for you.

their ghosts haunt me
as i walk that narrow hallway.
yet, i can't bring myself
to bury the remains of what
is still so cherished to me-

even after you gave up on us.

RETURN

your touch has become
strange to me;
foreign.

it's as if your American hands
once had a fantasy of learning the culture
passed down through my
child-bearing hips,
the intelligentsia reverberating
within my modicum of a voice,
the insecurities drawn
into the bags under my eyes
and slumped shoulders
that carry burdens unspoken.

it's as if tracing my
dry, brown, smooth skin
is a trek through uncharted terrain-
you see where it's going,
but you are unsure
what lies beyond the horizon.

NOBODY

nobody wants to be my anything
let alone
my everything

EYEPIECE

i almost cried.
you almost made me feel
loved
needed
desired
in ways that you've never expressed.

sex wasn't new to us

but for the first time,
i made love to you;
the smile on your face
penetrated me and held
my heart captive.

i can't feel that
outside of your presence.

i almost love you.

ZENITH

i may not be the most analytical
or intelligent person you will meet

but one thing i will tell you
is that you will not put
piss in a jar
and convince me that it

ain't piss

HISTOGRAM

i never thought you would
be so responsible as to
take my ailing heart,
so fragile and tender,
and make tattoos out of scars.
then again,
i also didn't realize
how much i had cut myself,
much less how deeply.

KELVIN MEASURED IN WERTS

when i was young
my grandmother smoked Newport 100s.
she'd buy them from the ice cream truck and from
Safeway. especially from CVS.

i'd smell the scent
of a freshly lit match
with the feeling of
pleasure coursing throughout my senses-
i inhaled it like cocaine.

i'd take her matchbook
when she drove grandpa to work,
and light match after match
after match after match
until the blue flames
and red charcoals
burned into crisp blackness.

i worked at CVS.
i took matches every day,
and struck them against
their homes, and watched them burn brilliantly-
so brightly, so beautifully, match after match
after match after match.

THE REAL ANTI MATTER

your daughter
whispers her face,
her sun caressed skin,
and brilliant mind's shine;

so whenever i unknowingly
flash the mile-wide smile
inherited from the woman
who bore your sorry ass,

when given the chance,
half of me mourns, solemnly,
and half of me stares in awe
at the wonder of genetics

DE MULE

the load y'all
placed upon my back
has curved my scoliosis-free spine into
an unanswerable question mark.

a hesitant smile
transforms into a painful grimace
as i unload my problems
and proverbial burdens
to pick up yours.

i wonder why y'all
treat me this way.

probably 'cuz you don't want
to know no better,
and don't care to
correct your wrongs.

INHALE, EXHALE

it's unfathomable
to do something as unpalatable
as admit when you're wrong
when you have no center.

i'm grounded now,
so i admit my flaws
as readily
as i own the gravity
of my strengths.

BLACK HOLE

everytime i
get the time to think of
ever
or never
having you
near
i
feel my
soul collapse into a
chocolate soaked
ice cream cone

ECLIPSE

your buttocks
are two moons
tumultuously engaging my
cerebrum
and
cerebellum
until i purge
my thoughts
into an endless summer

your clitoris is
the addiction
that crack could only wish
it could be

DARK ADAPTATION

once upon a time labels were great for
naming what we were
then,
just like capitalism,
they coiled their bodies around us and
became the cobra-like venom
emblazoning our animosity

CULMINATION

i thought about how inconsequential
my life would be without you.

i thought that doing everything to keep you around
would make you stay.

i thought that living independent of your desires
would leave me defenseless.

then i opened my third eye and saw that the

God you are does not detract

from the God i am.

we just rule differently.
and that's okay.

BARRED SPIRAL

i've started using drugs again-
the ones that let me see the nuances
and textures of the universe.

i've started using the ones that
open my mind to the possibilities
that we are simple beings
in a world devoid of order
and filled with colors
and body parts
that make it impossible
to remove oneself
from the other pieces
of oneself.

i've started using drugs again-
the ones that make me question
whether the universe exists
within the drugs
or without.

HEAVEN

LANGUAGE IN THEIR EYES:

THE APPROPRIATENESS OF SPEAKIN' FROM DE SOUTH

Zora Neale Hurston uses both Standard American English (SAE) and southern African American Vernacular English (AAVE) in *Their Eyes Were Watching God*.

I believe that the utilization of these two in direct contrast with one another was intentional; the usage of Standard American English in a narrative form versus the African American Vernacular English in the dialectical form is representative of the dichotomy of America and Black America. The narrator's language was formal, descriptive, grammatically, and technically correct. The way the narrator spoke is what is seen as proper and correct. In America, this is the standard, hence the name Standard American English.

The characters, however, used language that was in opposition to this; they used "*de*" instead of "the" and "*dem*" instead of "them." They also used dialectical language that was indicative of how they spoke in that particular region. For example, instead of saying "*sixty acres of land right on the big road,*" Janie's grandmother said "sixty acres uh land right on de big road" (Hurston 23). Hurston's use of "*uh*" versus "of" and "*de*" as opposed to "the" was to bridge the gap between the way language is written and the way it is spoken. According to an article in *Language and Literature*, there is definitely something to be said about "Hurston's constant attention to respelling words in order to reflect syllable-initial and syllable-final fricative stopping, a feature that is typically associated with varieties of AAVE" (Barry 182).

Another reason that Hurston uses African American Vernacular English in the dialect of the characters is to maintain authenticity. Published during the Harlem Renaissance, I believe that Hurston consciously participated in the celebration of Blackness. In exemplifying a particular section of southern American Blackness, she expressed "accuracy and sophistication" (Barry 182) in characters who would otherwise remain underrepresented. As can be seen from the text, even those characters who were not educated in the traditional sense had the curiosity, self-awareness, and yearning for liberation that their White counterparts had (Hurston 14). In many of the other texts we've read, it seems that Renaissance writers – such as Hurston, Dunbar, and Hughes – showed a shift in writing that actually reveled in the speaking patterns that Blacks had collectively.

In addition to the collective Black community that Hurston presented her work to in the real world, the porch that existed in *Their Eyes Were Watching God* was representative of the community – and lack thereof – in Janie's hometown of Eatonville. From the very beginning of the book, we see several women on the porch relaxing and spreading gossip. The text informs us that "these sitters had been tongueless, earless, eyeless conveniences all day. Mules and other brutes had occupied their skins. But now, the sun and the bossman were gone, so the skins felt powerful and human" (Hurston 1). The porch was a communal place to go after being worked all day long like an animal. Here, they were able to have control over how they spoke and what they spoke about, were able to rest their weary feet, and were able to lay their burdens down onto their fellow Black sistren. Janie's porch was more of a place of intimacy and peace. She and Phoeby were able to move away from the chaos and gossip of the other women, and it is here that Phoeby learned the private affairs of Janie, as well as her three husbands and the impact that her parents and grandmother had on her life.

Hurston's deliberate use of SAE and AAVE, combined with the women of the novel, ultimately were used to evoke a sense of community during an era of stimulation and growth of Black consciousness. Hurston's inclusion of southern African American Vernacular English that was written in a way that was authentic to the phonetic pronunciation of Eatonville, Florida was even more of an effort to destroy the idea of language as a monolith, and to push the linguistic difference of Blacks to the forefront.

Works Cited

Barry, Betsy. "'It's Hard Fuh Me To Understand What You Mean, De Way You Tell It': Representing Language in Zora Neale Hurston's Their Eyes Were Watching God." *Language and Literature* 10.2 (2001): 171-186.

Hurston, Zora Neale. *Their Eyes Were Watching God: A Novel*. New York: Perennial Library, 1990. Print.

WHEN WILL I KNOW

Today you looked at me with
serendipitous eyes—
Eyes that seemed unfazed by
trauma and pain.
Eyes that were unyielding and
unfathomably kind.
Eyes that shook my heart
to its core—
eyes that felt like home.
Eyes that knew that my nomadic
ways needed a rest.
That my feet were tired,
And my soul, weary.
So they held me.
And warmed me.
And never let me go.

INFINITESIMAL

Doubt and love cannot coexist
where our palsm, lips, and souls gather /
Every moment /
Every breath /
Every second I spend with you
makes being finite a privilege /

I will always be reminded that
art is created /
In negative space /
And you are the Grace Jones
meets Faith Ringgold
meets Kara Walker /

I scrutinize every chin hair /
Unkempt coil /
And freckle /
Only to come to the same conclusion /

I love you /
And that can't be quantified.

CONVICTION

I'm not one to speak
exceptionally loud if I don't feel
compelled to.
The find black hair sprouting from my
melanated skin
and my kinky, coiled crown
does that for me.
The lack of a need to present
a shell of myself
speaks for itself.

I am myself nearly 99% of the time...

...However...

What you ain't gonna do
is contort my love, passion, and loyalty
into the ugliness of contentment
and self-deprecating existentialism.

JUST IN CASE

I haven't told you today

I love you

And you will always have me

Whenever you need me

PROTECTION

If Black women are the home
And protect the peace of mind,
Black men are the fences
That keep the looters out
And the lovers in.

At least that's what I've been told.

I've never experienced that sentiment.

FULL

You are a harvest—
a cornucopia of necessity
and gluttony—
that I can never over
or under
consume

YOUR SCENT

tastes just as good as it did
when we first met

see, i was feeling you
before i was feeling you,

and you dripping in my mouth
is just the drizzle of honey

with the sweet, sweet undertones
of pheromones

that i need to start off my day

UNBORN

i'm so sorry for the
world that i exist in.
i can't protect you from the
horrors
humans
hellfire and brimstone
that exists on this rock,
and because of that
i refuse to let those things,
or myself,
even as a God,
hurt you
in any way.
i'd never forgive myself.
and thus
i'll mourn you.
forever.

ENLIGHTENMENT

Enlightenment,
At this point in my life,
Feels like knowing what is right
And doing what is right
Without a second guess.

Peace,
At this point in my life,
Feels like making plans
And breaking plans,
because I need a long, deep rest.

URBAN RHAPSODY

Your spirit is musical
Appearance is beautiful
You keep it a hunnit
No ego or nothin
Rhapsody's ain't new to you

Your theses are immutable
And you're all over Google, too
With these moves you're making
I can't even fake it
My intrigue is unusual

STARDUST

www.ingramcontent.com/pod-product-compliance
Lightning Source LLC
Chambersburg PA
CBHW041325110526
44592CB00021B/2823